No Backbone!
The World of Invertebrates

Smelly Stink Bugs

by Meish Goldish

Consultant: Brian V. Brown
Curator, Entomology Section
Natural History Museum of Los Angeles County

BEARPORT PUBLISHING

NEW YORK, NEW YORK

Credits

Cover, 4–5, © Ingo Arndt/Minden Pictures; 6–7, © NHPA/James Carmichael Jr; 8T, © Mark Moffett/Minden Pictures; 8M, © Art Wolfe/Riser/Getty Images; 8B, © Ingo Arndt/Minden Pictures; 9, © Clemson University-USDA Cooperative Extension Slide Series, Bugwood.org; 10, © David Kuhn/Dwight Kuhn Photography; 11, © Jack Clark/ Animals Animals Earth Scenes; 12, © NHPA/James Carmichael Jr; 13, © Ed Reschke/Peter Arnold, Inc.; 14–15, © Nick Monaghan; 16, © Piotr Naskrecki/Minden Pictures; 17, © David Kuhn/Dwight Kuhn Photography; 18, © Doug Wechsler/The Academy of Natural Sciences; 19, © David R. Lance, USDA APHIS PPQ, United States; 20, © Lynette Schimming; 21, © Ingo Arndt/Minden Pictures; 22TL, © Dwight Kuhn/Dwight Kuhn Photography; 22TR, © Oxford Scientific Films/Photolibrary; 22BL, © Tom Murray/BugGuide.com; 22BR, © Tom Murray/BugGuide.com; 22Spot, © Whitney Cranshaw, Colorado State University, Bugwood.org; 23TL, © Jim Wehtje/Photodisc Green/Getty Images; 23TR, © Jack Clark/Animals Animals Earth Scenes; 23BL, © Kevin D. Arvin, United States; 23BR, © David R. Lance, USDA APHIS PPQ, United States.

Publisher: Kenn Goin
Editorial Director: Adam Siegel
Creative Director: Spencer Brinker
Design: Dawn Beard Creative
Photo Researcher: Nancy Tobin

Library of Congress Cataloging-in-Publication Data

Goldish, Meish.
  Smelly stink bugs / by Meish Goldish.
    p. cm. — (No backbone! The world of invertebrates)
  Includes bibliographical references and index.
  ISBN-13: 978-1-59716-580-8 (library binding)
  ISBN-10: 1-59716-580-8 (library binding)
  1. Stinkbugs—Juvenile literature. I. Title.

QL523.P5G65 2008
595.7—dc22

                    2007031228

For more information, write to Bearport Publishing Company, Inc., 101 Fifth Avenue, Suite 6R, New York, New York 10003. Printed in the United States of America.

10 9 8 7 6 5 4 3 2

Contents

Making a Stink

A stink bug is a kind of **insect**.

It gets its name from the stinky liquid it makes in its body.

When a stink bug is scared, it sprays the liquid—and it smells awful!

Some people call stink bugs the skunks of the insect world.

5

A Skeleton on the Outside

Like all insects, a stink bug has six legs and two antennas.

It also has a hard covering called an exoskeleton.

This kind of skeleton is on the outside of an insect's body.

The exoskeleton protects the soft parts of the stink bug's body.

Many kinds of animals use their noses to smell things. Stink bugs don't have noses. They use their antennas for smelling.

legs

antennas

7

Pretty Colors

Stink bugs can smell bad, but they can also look pretty.

Some are bright green.

Others are bright red.

One of the most colorful kinds is black with red, orange, or yellow marks.

There are more than 4,000 kinds of stink bugs.

9

A Needle-Sharp Beak

A stink bug has a long **beak** at the front of its head.

The beak has four thin needles inside.

A hungry stink bug sticks the needles into its food to eat.

beak

When a stink bug is not eating, it tucks its beak under its body.

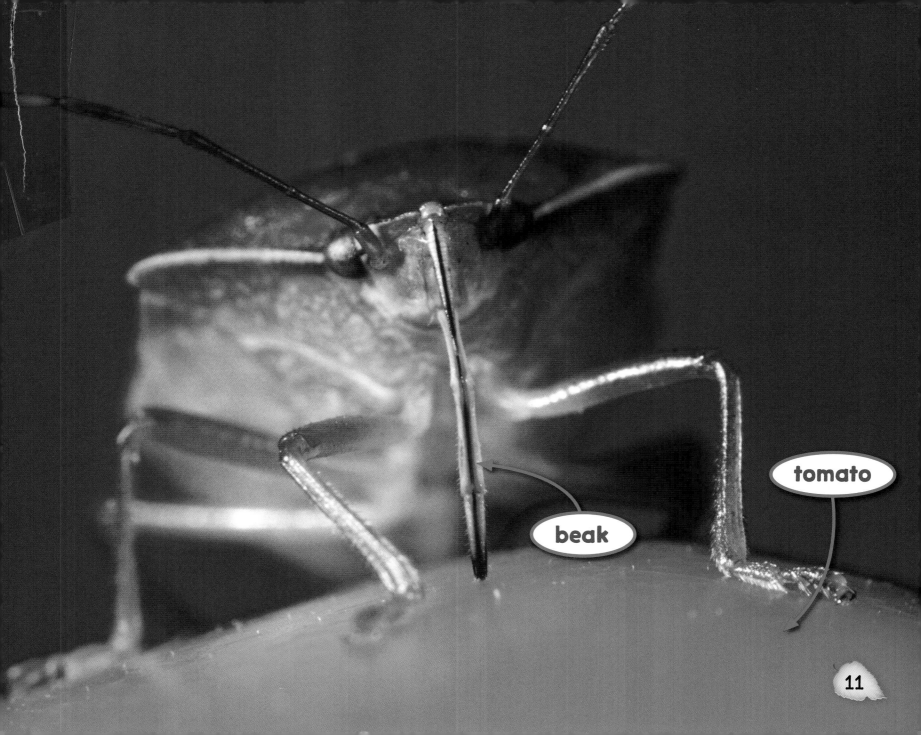

beak

tomato

A Liquid Diet

Stink bugs can't chew food.

Instead, they use their beaks like straws to suck up liquids.

Most stink bugs suck the juice from plants.

Some stink bugs suck blood from the bodies of other insects.

Some kinds of stink bugs like to suck on bean and tomato plants. Others like to suck on cabbage.

fruit

12

caterpillar

Stinky Meals

A stink bug's bad smell protects it from being eaten.

The bug sprays its stinky liquid when an enemy comes near.

The enemy usually goes away.

Some insects, birds, and spiders will eat the smelly bugs, however.

Stink bugs not only smell bad, they taste bad, too. Many birds bite into stink bugs and then spit them out.

robber fly

stink bug

15

Blending In

Some stink bugs depend on more than their bad smell to stay safe.

They also depend on their color.

The bugs blend in with the plants around them.

Their enemies can't see them easily.

Green stink bugs blend in with leaves. Brown stink bugs blend in with tree bark.

Starting Out

Baby stink bugs start out as eggs.

The babies that hatch from the eggs are called **nymphs**.

Each nymph is the shape of an adult stink bug, only smaller and without wings.

A mother stink bug usually lays her eggs on plant leaves. She can lay up to 500 eggs at a time.

eggs

eggs

nymphs

Growing Up

A stink bug nymph is born with an exoskeleton, but this covering cannot get bigger.

As the nymph grows, it sheds its old exoskeleton so that a new one can form.

This change is called molting.

A growing nymph molts five times in all.

Then the stink bug is an adult, ready to make a big stink of its own!

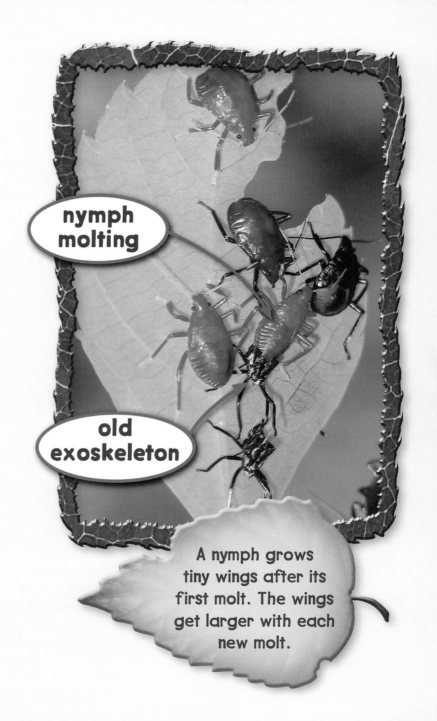

nymph molting

old exoskeleton

A nymph grows tiny wings after its first molt. The wings get larger with each new molt.

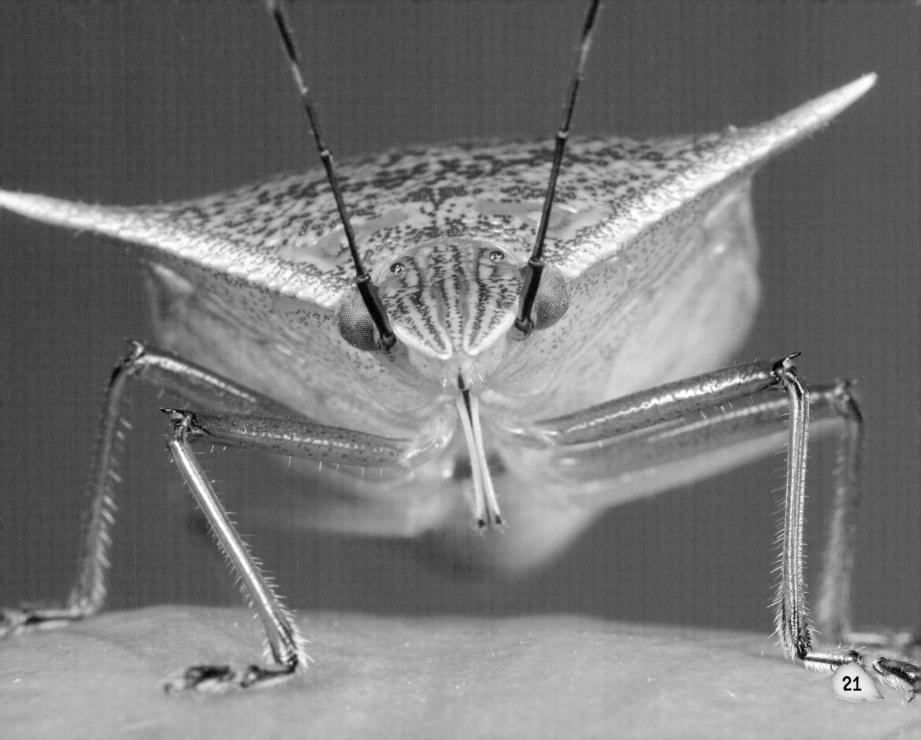

A World of Invertebrates

An animal that has a skeleton with a **backbone** inside its body is a *vertebrate* (VUR-tuh-brit). Mammals, birds, fish, reptiles, and amphibians are all vertebrates.

An animal that does not have a skeleton with a backbone inside its body is an *invertebrate* (in-VUR-tuh-brit). More than 95 percent of all kinds of animals on Earth are invertebrates.

Some invertebrates, such as insects and spiders, have hard skeletons—called exoskeletons—outside their bodies. Other invertebrates, such as worms and jellyfish, have soft, squishy bodies with no exoskeletons to protect them.

Here are four insects that are closely related to stink bugs. Like all insects, they are invertebrates.

Squash Bug

Bed Bug

Chinch Bug

Flat Bug

Glossary

backbone (BAK-*bohn*) a group of connected bones that run along the backs of some animals, such as dogs, cats, and fish; also called a spine

beak (BEEK) the long, thin part of a stink bug's mouth used to suck liquid from plants or other insects

insect (IN-sekt) a small animal that has six legs, three main body parts, two antennas, and a hard covering called an exoskeleton

nymphs (NIMFS) young insects that change into adults by growing and shedding their exoskeleton again and again

Index

Read More

Hughes, Monica. *Bugs.* New York: Bearport Publishing (2006).

Kravetz, Jonathan. *Stink Bugs.* New York: Rosen Publishing Group (2006).

Learn More Online

To learn more about stink bugs, visit

www.bearportpublishing.com/NoBackbone-Insects

About the Author

Meish Goldish has written more than 100 books for children.
He lives in Brooklyn, New York.